Series editor
ALISTAIR
BRYCE-CLEGG

fantastic ideas for
treasure baskets

SUE GASCOYNE

Featherstone
An imprint of Bloomsbury Publishing Plc

50 Bedford Square
London
WC1B 3DP
UK

1385 Broadway
New York
NY 10018
USA

www.bloomsbury.com

FEATHERSTONE and the Feather logo are trademarks of Bloomsbury Publishing Plc

First published in Great Britain 2017

A catalogue record for this book is available from the British Library.

ISBN
PB: 978-1-4729-4351-4
ePDF: 978-1-4729-4350-7

2 4 6 8 10 9 7 5 3 1

Printed and bound in India by Replika Press Pvt. Ltd.

This book is produced using paper that is made from wood grown in managed, sustainable forests.
It is natural, renewable and recyclable. The logging and manufacturing processes conform to the
environmental regulations of the country of origin.

To find out more about our authors and books visit www.bloomsbury.com. Here you will find extracts,
author interviews, details of forthcoming events and the option to sign up for our newsletters.

Acknowledgements
Thanks to Amelia, Andra, Andrew, Charlotte, Daniel, Freddie, Freya, Harrison, Indie, Jacob,
Joanna, Jude, Lara, Leah, Maria, Santiago, Sinead and Zach for sharing their play and
a special thank you to staff and children at Springlands Nursery.

Contents

What is a Treasure Basket?

A Treasure Basket is essentially a collection of sensory-rich natural and household objects, carefully picked to offer children limitless play possibilities, offered in a basket. Although originally developed by Elinor Goldschmied in the 1940s to captivate infants not yet walking, one only has to watch children's exploration of an assortment of well-chosen open-ended objects to see that they are equally fascinating to older children.

Treasure Baskets were designed to provide babies with opportunities to play freely with objects, exploring and manipulating them with no adult direction or involvement. As such, a book like this offering 50 activity ideas may seem at odds with Goldschmied's original idea. In fact, both the author and this book recognise the value of children using this resource for free play. With access to sensory resources and environments ever decreasing, now more than ever it is essential to give children ample opportunities to freely explore the sensory-rich treasures of a Treasure Basket, manipulating them, developing working theories and testing ideas.

Sensory Play Continuum

Many early years practitioners and parents struggle with their role in supporting Treasure Basket play or may feel uncomfortable with the idea of not directing or being actively involved. With this in mind the author developed the Sensory Play Continuum (Gascoyne, 2009), a useful tool for supporting adults with the practice of when and when not to intervene in children's play to achieve a balance between adult and child-led activities.

Obstacles to Treasure Basket play

Common obstacles to getting the most out of Treasure Basket play include confusion over:

- Whom to offer Treasure Baskets to
- How to offer this resource and what the adult's role is
- What to include and why.

We will now look at each of these in turn.

Stage	Type of play	Adult's role	Where in book
Stage 1	Free play with a Treasure Basket	Provide a stimulating resource and record and notice play.	Activity 1
Stage 2	The child chooses whether and how to use the objects with other resources, (such as sand and water) for free play	As Stage 1 but offer another open-ended resource for the child to combine if wished.	Activity 2
Stage 3	Adult-initiated activity using the objects (such as sinking and floating)	Introduce an activity and support thinking and questions.	Activities 3-50

Whom to offer Treasure Baskets to

Although originally intended for babies, enlightened parents and practitioners have witnessed the appeal of Treasure Baskets for children aged up to six years and even older. This is also a great tool for supporting children with SEN. The three stages of the Sensory Play Continuum, and types of activities set out in this book, enable older children to access and enjoy the huge play and learning potential of Treasure Baskets.

How to use or offer this resource and what the adult's role is

Sometimes the biggest obstacle to play can be adults not appreciating the potential of an object as a valuable play and learning resource. With so many toys offering limited freedom and play value, a carefully-chosen collection of resources, such as those found in a good quality Treasure Basket, enables children to use the objects in limitless ways. This makes them very attractive for children to explore their ideas, discover things about the world and themselves, and develop preferences and mastery.

Left to their own devices, children of all ages will happily play with and explore a stimulating Treasure Basket for extended periods of time, developing their gross motor skills as they sit and reach for objects; fine motor skills and hand-eye coordination as they select objects; and focus, concentration, and well-being as they pursue their interests and ideas. The adult's vital role in supporting this type of play is selecting the stimulating objects and providing the necessary space, permission, and time for children to freely explore and immerse themselves in their investigations.

Ideally two to five year olds should be offered the Treasure Basket in a quiet space on the floor. The adult should sit nearby watching explorations but not directing or commentating on play. The adult unobtrusively puts any 'discarded' treasures back in the basket to enable children to easily access them.

What to include and why

A common challenge is understanding what to include in a Treasure Basket. If each object is carefully picked for its special qualities, children of all ages will be captivated and excited by this resource. However, if the objects are not sensory-rich, carefully chosen and scaled to fit a child's hand, then a Treasure Basket can quickly start to resemble an 'odds-and-ends bin'. This will dilute its impact and appeal and often means the resource fails to stimulate children's interest and attention, perhaps reinforcing the idea that Treasure Baskets are 'just for babies'.

What sorts of objects should be included in a Treasure Basket?

- Remember the aim is to offer as much **variety and sensory interest** as possible, being aware of the importance of safety. A Treasure Basket offers a welcome alternative to children's often plastic-dominated life, so it's important to include objects with different textures, detail, colours, shapes, weight, and sizes.

- All the objects should be **scaled** to suit child-size hands.

- Include a mix of **familiar objects** that children may recognise from home or outdoors and some **unusual objects** that will offer excitement, awe, and wonder.

- Include a mix of **everyday objects** made from wood, metal, stone, wicker, rubber, fabric, and cardboard.

- Include some **natural resources** such as an interesting sturdy shell, cobblestone or pine cone.

- A selection of **utensil-shaped objects**, great for manipulating, stirring, etc.

- A variety of **containers** for putting things in, as children love the surprise of discovering things. Include a wide selection of shapes and types of materials.

The following objects would make a good start to your own Treasure Basket collection and work well in the activities.

Containers – e.g. A tin, mini terracotta pot, mini cardboard box, purse, pot, mini bowl, or colander.

Utensils – e.g. A teaspoon, short wooden spoon, measuring spoons, tongs, juicer, dolly peg, tea strainer, robust whisk, pastry brush.

Natural objects – e.g. A cobblestone, robust shell, pine cone, wicker ball, loofah, or hoop.

Miscellaneous – e.g. A variety of balls, fabric items, mini beanbags, a chain, plug, lavender bag, mini board book

What will two to five year olds learn when they play with the objects in a Treasure Basket or collection of sensory-rich objects?

You can expect to see children engaging in a wealth of exploration, manipulation and trial and error investigation as they test out their ideas, develop interests and reshape their working theories about the world around them. Typically Treasure Basket play offers the following cross-curricular benefits:

PSED – Increases self-esteem, self-occupation, sense of mastery, well-being, focus and concentration

Physical development – Develops fine and gross motor skills and strength and tool use

Communication and language – Supports listening, attention, turn-taking, imagination and stimulates language

Mathematics – Introduces shape, measure, number, pattern, sorting, weight, symmetry, and volume

Literacy – Gives meaning to words and 'wow' factor, inspires rich language

Understanding the world – Supports understanding of properties and how things work

Expressive arts and design – Encourages creativity and inspires imagination.

I've heard of heuristic play. What's the difference between this and a Treasure Basket?

Typically, heuristic or 'discovery' play involves multiple objects picked for their numbers and commonality, rather than individuality and sensory appeal. Children play in a trial and error way with collections of balls, hoops, and containers, etc., choosing if and how to use the resources together. Treasure Baskets, in contrast, are made up of a wide variety of individual items with no duplication, and children choose whether to explore the resources, use them for heuristic play, or for imaginative play.

A word about safety...

Objects need to be robust, with no sharp edges or small parts that could cause a potential hazard. Avoid painted or varnished objects unless you know for sure that they are child-safe. Remember that the children will be handling and possibly even mouthing the objects, so if in doubt always err on the side of caution.

Introducing the activities

As adults play such a key role in maximising the benefits of Treasure Basket play, the first three activities are designed to give adults the chance to experience the awe and wonder of a Treasure Basket, either in a group or on their own.

The structure of the book

The pages are all organised in the same way. Before you start any activity, read through everything on the page so you are familiar with the whole activity and what you might need to plan in advance.

What you need lists the resources required for the activity. These are likely to be readily available in most settings or can be bought easily.

What to do tells you step-by-step what you need to do to compete the activity.

Top tips give a brief suggestion or piece of advice to help in tackling the individual activity – these are things we wish we had known before we did them!

The **Health & Safety** tips are often obvious, but safety can't be overstressed. In many cases there are no specific hazards involved in completing the activity, and your usual health and safety measures should be enough. In others there are particular issues to be noted and addressed.

Taking it forward gives ideas for additional activities on the same theme, or for developing the activity further. These will be particularly useful for things that have gone especially well or where children show a real interest. In many cases they use the same resources, and in every case they have been designed to extend learning and broaden the children's experiences.

What's in it for the children? tells you (and others) briefly how the suggested activities contribute to learning.

Vocabulary flags the key terms to use during the activity to encourage language development.

A sensory journey
Stage 1 Sensory Play Continuum

What you need:

- A Treasure Basket – if you do not already have one, follow the guidance on page six to assemble a basket of non-plastic objects. If doing this in a group, invite individuals to each bring two objects from home or outdoors, to include

- Two fabric bags or pillow cases

- A selection of toys

- Sticky notes and A5 cards.

Top tip

The objects within a Treasure Basket are designed to be enjoyed both on their own and together. Each child will have their own favourite objects. Explore your own personal preferences by picking an object.

Taking it forward

- Challenge individuals to try to find one or more unusual objects to bring in that others may not recognise. Guess what each object might be, and then when revealed, talk about how a collection of objects must feel to children for whom many of the treasures are mystery objects.

- Write the following essentials for Treasure Basket objects on a card: **Variety, Sensory interest, Safe, Child-scale.**

- Invite individuals to sort through the Treasure Basket objects, placing any that meet these requirements on the table, discussing any differences of opinion.

- Agree any actions needed for those objects not selected.

What to do:

1. Empty the contents of the Treasure Basket into one feely bag and the toys into another.

2. Individually or in groups of up to four, take it in turns feeling in the two bags. List any describing words that come to mind and record on separate sticky notes. Continue until everyone has had a chance to feel in both bags.

3. Tip the contents out and talk about the two sets of words, inviting each group to share those they find most striking.

4. Discuss what is similar and different about these and share any surprises or feelings about what felt different about the two bags.

5. Put the treasures into the basket and write on separate cards the five external senses of touch, sight, sound, smell, and taste. Invite the group to sort the Treasure Basket objects according to which senses they most appeal to.

6. Discuss the findings and compare. Treasures should be picked for their sensory interest, so if people struggled to identify sensory qualities, reconsider the basket contents.

One and one makes fun

What you need:

- A Treasure Basket or collection of objects
- A sand tray or container ideally containing a mix of dry sand, dried rice, lentils, and glitter
- A water tray or container (ice cubes and glitter optional).

Top tip ⭐

- Add a playdough and clay 'station' too with a selection of wooden and metal treasures.

- From infancy, children are naturally drawn to novelty, pattern and detail which is why collections of objects offer so much appeal. They are strongly motivated to try to understand how things work, spot differences and similarities between objects and don't tend to be constrained like adults, which makes them naturally creative and divergent thinkers. Offering open-ended resources together enables children to satisfy their natural drive to discover.

Taking it forward

- A Treasure Basket should be provided in a quiet space in or outdoors, without adult commentary or involvement. Children should have long enough to become absorbed. Share how you felt when the activity ended: would you ideally have liked more time? If anyone has comments about being interrupted or disturbed by the noise of others, discuss these also. Reflect on what children might be experiencing and whether changes to existing practice are needed.

What to do:

1. Set up two or three sensory stations in different areas of the room and position a selection of treasures, such as different-sized wooden and metal spoons, pots, funnels, and tea strainers next to each tray.

2. In groups spend time exploring and playing with the resources, quietly noticing how they feel. Observe and enjoy the different textures and sensations and how they make you feel. Ideally this should be carried out in silence or quiet contemplation.

3. Once everyone has experienced both (or all three stations) talk about what they noticed, their feelings and any surprises.

4. Discuss if and how combining the resources changed or enhanced play. List any learning points about these key areas of provision.

What you need:

- A Treasure Basket
- Water tray
- Balancing scales

Top tip

The objects in a Treasure Basket are perfect for a host of scientific investigations because their unique qualities make it much more difficult to accurately predict what will happen. This helps level the playing field between adult's and children's knowledge and forces adults to reappraise their existing thinking which makes for much more exciting adult/child interactions.

Taking it forward

- Sit in a circle around the Treasure Basket. Pick an object and explain that the challenge is to come up with as many different uses for the object as possible. These can be imaginary, silly, or real.

- Pass the object around the circle as people say a use. Alternatively, put the object in the centre of the circle for people to pick up when they have an idea to share.

- Increase the challenge by miming a use instead, or playing in teams or against the clock to introduce healthy competition and fun.

- Talk about which of the three stages of the Sensory Play Continuum (free play, free play with other resources, or the adult-initiated activity) they most enjoyed? Did each stage offer different benefits, appeal and learning opportunities?

What to do:

1. Create two activity stations: one with the balancing scales and the other with the water tray. Arrange an assortment of objects next to each.

2. Follow the activities on page 14 and 56, using these as a springboard for exploring the resources, to discover which objects sink/float and which objects are heaviest/lightest.

3. Predict what will happen if the objects are put in water or measured.

4. Discuss any surprises, for example some wooden spoons may sink, others float and still others lie diagonally! Some fabrics may weigh a lot more than you think!

Air writing

What you need:

- A selection of scarves or flannel-sized pieces of fabric, enough for one (or two) for each child. Try to pick a variety of fabrics, e.g. silky, floaty, transparent, towelling, patterned, plain
- Basket or box for cloths
- A selection of songs in a range of tempos and a way of playing them.

Top tip

This multi-sensory activity will appeal to kinaesthetic learners who would struggle to sit still with pen and paper.

Taking it forward

- Play outdoors for a science focus on wind direction.
- Provide pegs and string for the children to use for a range of projects, such as making tents, parachute games or laundry/fabric shop role-plays.

What's in it for the children?

Develops gross and fine motor skills and an awareness of letters and shapes in preparation for writing. Encourages an awareness of the child's own body, rhythm and space, and calms or re-energises.

Vocabulary

Introduce: arc, drop, float, flow, quickly, slowly, spin, stretch, swirl, twirl, waft, wave etc.

➕ Health & Safety

Ensure there is enough space to avoid collisions.

What to do:

1. The children pick a cloth to hold and find a space to stand in.

2. Encourage them to swirl and twirl the cloth as they move their arms to gently warm-up.

3. Play music with a range of tempos for the children to move freely and explore the crescendos and lulls of the rhythm. Vary by inviting them to move carefully around the room (or outdoor area).

4. Model making large movements that cross the midline (an imaginary vertical line down the centre of the body) as this helps the left and right hemispheres of the brain work better together and energises children ready for learning.

5. Challenge them to 'write' their name in the air with their cloth, like a plane doing a loop the loop or a sparkler. Support, if needed, by moving the child's hand to form the letters. Vary the music tempo to add interest and vary speed.

6. Use for action songs, 'What am I doing?' or 'Who am I?' (the children try to guess an action or animal) or a game of follow the leader, (someone picks an action or animal, such as an elephant's trunk, to make with the cloth for others to copy).

Balancing act

What you need:

- A Treasure Basket or collection of everyday household objects and natural treasures
- Balancing scales and weights
- Metric scales, if desired

Top tip

Initially pick objects with widely contrasting weights so that the weight difference is obvious. Increase the challenge by picking objects with similar weights.

Taking it forward

- Challenge them to find the heaviest/lightest object or things that weigh the same.

- Invite them to use the weights to try to balance the arms of the scales and start to put a figure on the weight difference. Provide play money for a shop role-play.

What's in it for the children?

Develops mathematical understanding, problem solving, balance and gross motor skills in a fun way.

Vocabulary

Introduce: balance, different, heavier, heavy, less, light, lighter, materials, more, properties, same, weigh.

What to do:

1. Invite the children to select one of the objects to put on each side of the balancing scales.

2. Point out how the arms move up and down as they balance, then invite the children to practise moving their arms up and down to balance like the scales. They may find that closing their eyes makes it easier.

3. Pick two objects and invite the children to guess which feels heavier.

4. Invite a child to become the scales by moving their arms up and down. The lighter the object, the higher the arm.

5. They can then check their guesses by using the scales and talk about any surprises as some things may weigh more than you expect!

6. Take it in turns predicting and balancing different objects.

7. If appropriate, children can sort the objects into two piles: one for heavier and one for lighter objects. They can then look at the objects and talk about why they think some objects might be heavier.

Box of delights

What you need:

- A cardboard box filled with shredded paper, maize packaging pieces, newspaper, or a mix of these
- Several different-shaped objects – either unusual objects with awe and wonder or familiar objects
- Sticky tape

Top tip

Capture children's interest by including a set kitchen timer or other noisy object that suddenly starts to ring. Try to use multi-coloured shredded paper for added interest.

Taking it forward

- Wrap the objects in newspaper instead for a game of pass the parcel. Each time the music stops, the children try to guess what the object is before taking off another layer of paper.

What's in it for the children?

Introduces tactile and sensory exploration, develops problem solving and manipulation.

Vocabulary

Introduce: inside, hidden, parcel, surprise (and lots of describing words).

 Health & Safety

Avoid polystyrene packaging which can be a choking hazard.

What to do:

1. Hide five or more objects in the box of packaging materials, seal the box and gather the children round.

2. Introduce the surprise parcel and invite them to help you open it to find out what's inside. Model being very careful in case the contents are fragile.

3. Enjoy feeling the packaging and objects while still in the box, and encourage them to guess what the objects are, for example 'I wonder if we can guess what's inside without looking?'

4. One at a time, the children can reveal the objects and talk about their guesses, what they think each object is, and any surprises.

Buried treasure

What you need:

- Some treasure-like objects such as a chunky chains, necklaces and metal or pottery pots
- A selection of brushes, scoops, and spoons (the more variety of size, shape, and material the better)
- A large cobblestone to represent a fossilised dinosaur egg
- Sand tray
- Hand-held magnets for a metal detector dig
- Magnifying glasses
- Cameras (optional)

What to do:

1. Secretly bury the stone and some treasure-like objects in the sand. Arrange the brushes and spoons next to the sand tray.

2. Gather the children around and ask if anyone has been to a museum and seen bones, bits of pots, coins and other things found in an archaeological dig. Ask/explain what an archaeological dig is – where archaeologists discover signs of the past, such as dinosaur bones and the pots and everyday things used by people from the past, such as the Romans. If possible, show pictures or better still, some real finds; or visit a display.

3. Exclaim that you've heard that a fossilised dinosaur 'egg' is buried in the sand and ask if they'd like to use the brushes and spoons to carefully search for it?

4. Model gently using a brush to reveal the base of the sand tray. Share children's delight in discovering more treasures and marvel about what they might be and where they have come from.

5. Use the magnifying glasses to explore the treasures in more detail.

6. Support the children in deciding what to do about the 'egg' and treasures, e.g. keeping the egg warm to see if it hatches, or displaying the treasures as if they were museum exhibits.

Taking it forward

- Secretly bury some metal objects in the sand for the children to discover when using hand-held magnets. Ask if any of the children have seen a metal detector in action; talk about their experience; then, one at a time, the children take it in turns to use a magnet to search for treasure.

- Experiment by burying all metal objects, a mix of metal and non-metal. Include some metals that do not attract, and talk about why the magnets worked with some objects but not others, being sure to use the correct language of attract and repulse. Magnets attract metals that have iron in them, e.g. steel and nickel. If appropriate, provide cameras for children to record the dig or capture their favourite finds.

What's in it for the children?

Develops hand-eye coordination, fine and gross motor skills and tool use. Encourages problem solving, scientific and critical thinking. Supports self-occupation, calms and increases self-esteem.

Vocabulary

Introduce: archaeological dig, attract, repulse, dinosaur, egg, exhibit, magnet, metal, museum, palaeontology, treasure.

Top tip ★

Try to pick a wide selection of brushes, scoops, and spoons, rather than multiples of one style, as this increases interest and develops problem solving, critical thinking, fine motor skills and tool use. Pastry and nail brushes work particularly well. Introduce after a visit to a museum or reading a story such as those in the *Harry and the Dinosaurs* series (I. Whybrow and A. Reynolds).

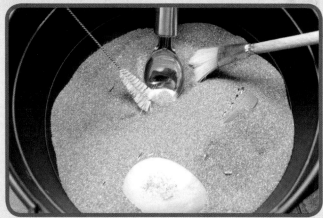

50 fantastic ideas for treasure baskets

Camo colours

What you need:

- A range of different-coloured wooden, metal, textile, rubber, and natural objects
- A sand tray and plain or coloured sand
- Water tray or bubble bath and food colouring
- Pop-up tent or dark den
- DIY colour swatches, torches, colour paddles, nets, spoons, and scoop

> **Top tip**
>
> Be sure to select objects that won't be ruined in water or sticky resources. These sensory colour provocations will enthral and captivate children.

What to do:

1. Create three or more sensory colour areas where children can explore colour. Pick the colours to match the objects. Examples could include:

   a. Natural and yellow objects in a sand tray (or if using coloured sand, the appropriate colour).

   b. Brown and red objects in a container of autumn leaves.

   c. Coloured water in a water tray (e.g. green, blue, or red) and matching coloured objects. Alternatively, add bubbles and ice cubes for opaque objects.

   d. Set up a pop-up tent in a dark space, cover the floor with a black or grey blanket, then position black or grey objects on this, with torches available.

2. Give the children ample time to explore the sensory provocations in a hands-on way.

3. Talk about their findings and any surprises.

4. Provide resources and books for children to explore colour mixing, transient art and camouflage further.

Taking it forward

- Provide other media such as dried rice or porridge oats, Gelli Baff or wood shavings for the children to explore with the objects and create their own transient colour art installations.

Vocabulary

Introduce: camouflage, change, colour, dark, different, hidden, hue, light, same, shade, texture, tint, tone.

Counting holes

What you need:

- An array of objects with holes such as a tea strainer, sieve, mini colander, tea infuser, funnel, set of measuring spoons, spoons with holes, knitted purse etc.
- Torches, binoculars, light box, diffractors, magnifiers, colour paddles and DIY colour swatch cards with view finders

Top tip ⭐

Set up tunnels for the children to shine the torches in and crawl through. Follow with a lunch of holey cheese or toad in the hole!

What to do:

1. Gather around and invite the children to explore the objects using the tools provided.

2. After plenty of time ask if they notice anything that the objects have in common, looking through one of the holes as a clue if needed.

3. Invite them to spot holes in and on the objects to see if they can find which object has the most or biggest holes. The torches and tools should help them spot tiny holes, so plan this activity in an area with good natural light as well as access to a dark space.

4. Talk about what makes a hole a hole and whether it must go all the way through.

5. If appropriate, they can estimate numbers. Talk about why they think the objects contain holes and what purpose these serve, if any.

6. Go on a hole hunt in or outdoors to see what other wonders the children find. Invite them to share their favourite, most unusual or funniest hole; or children can suggest their own categories.

Taking it forward

- Go on a visit to spot holes in local buildings.
- Read *The Biggest Hole in the World* (P. Little and S. Hanson, 2006).
- Dig a mud pit together for a wealth of exploration.

What's in it for the children?

Develops creative thinking, observational skills, counting, estimation and tool use.

Vocabulary

Introduce: big, hole, holey, long, narrow, perforations, short, small, wide, etc.

Colour match

What you need:

- A collection of sensory-rich objects picked for their varied colours and detail

- Enough DIY colour swatches for individual or paired work

- A5 cards, each with colours written and painted on them (optional)

- Several colour-themed table covers, such as red berries, yellow bananas, wallpaper or wrapping paper (optional)

- PE hoops or string for sorting (optional)

What to do:

1. Spread the colour swatches on the floor and invite the children to try to find objects that match each colour.

2. Alternatively, put the cards in a pile face down and invite the children, one at a time, to take a card off the pile and try to find the matching object.

3. Talk about the different colours and any surprises as they find matching objects or struggle to do so.

4. Use the colour/word cards and PE hoops (or string arranged in circles) for children to sort the objects. Talk about the range of shades and which colours children like best and why.

5. Add movement and excitement by positioning different colour 'stations' around the room or outside area. Children pick a card and find a matching object which they position on the relevant colour station.

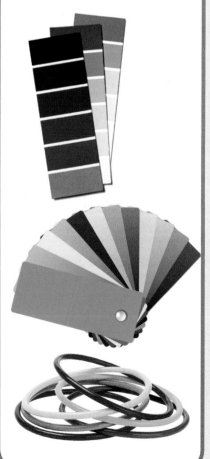

Top tip ⭐

Many DIY stores have individual colour swatch cards, complete with viewing windows. These are ideal for looking through and colour matching. Pick a range of colours to complement the collection of objects and environment, e.g. greys for a pebbly beach, greens for foliage or reds for bricks or autumnal leaves. Laminate for re-use.

Taking it forward

- Invite each child to pick a colour swatch to take on a colour hunt indoors, either individually or in pairs. Repeat outdoors, then talk about any surprises, what was easy or difficult and why.

- Older children can play a version of snap using the objects and cards instead.

- Talk about whether some colours make them think of particular feelings, such as yellow for happy, red for angry. Invite them to pick a colour that represents how they feel.

What's in it for the children?

Helps develop an awareness of the wide range of colours in the environment and the potential for colour mixing. Encourages attention to detail, focus and concentration. Introduces likes, dislikes, and feelings.

Vocabulary

Introduce: bright, colour, dark, hue, light, mix, pigment, primary, secondary, shade, tint, tone.

➕ **Health & Safety**

Reinforce rules about not picking up natural treasures such as berries (which could be poisonous) and the importance of washing hands afterwards.

Detectives

What to do:

1. Arrange the ten objects in the basket on the floor.

2. Prepare picture and word cards (written in lower case) for a range of recognisable shape characteristics (e.g. straight side, curve, one corner, three corners, four corners).

3. Shuffle the cards and place face down in a pile.

4. Children take it in turns picking a card from the top of the pile and finding a matching object from the basket.

5. Provide support if needed by summarising, e.g. 'So you're looking for an object with one straight side…'.

6. If the child finds a matching object, they keep the object and put the card at the bottom of the pile, continuing until the basket is empty. The aim is to collect the most objects.

7. Play in teams and introduce a points system, such as two points for an object from the basket, one point if from the room.

Top tip ⭐

Support younger children by selecting only those objects which are easily-recognisable shapes or have obvious characteristics. Add challenge for older children by writing cards with more detail (e.g. one curve and one straight line, two curves, or actual shapes).

circle   curve

Taking it forward

- Play in teams or against the clock. Vary by picking out all the objects that match each card. Provide magnifiers for the children to examine the objects in detail, spotting characteristics within and on the objects too.

What's in it for the children?

Recognising the different characteristics of shapes supports mathematical thinking and lays the foundations for writing.

Vocabulary

Introduce: circle, corner, curve, different, less, more, numbers, same, shapes, square, straight.

Down the tube

What you need:

- **An assortment of tubing of different lengths and diameters** (kitchen towel rolls, wrapping paper rolls, cardboard poster tubes and guttering would all work well)
- **A collection of everyday objects** (these should vary in size, weight, and solidity)
- **Two toy cars**

Taking it forward

- Fill several containers with an assortment of different resources (e.g. flour, jelly, shredded paper, dried rice, etc.) for the objects to fall in. Arrange on a protective mat, or play outside, so that the children can fully explore speed and displacement.

What's in it for the children?

Supports children's tracking skills and hand-eye coordination, both of which are necessary for reading and writing. Develops problem solving, mathematical and scientific thinking and fine and gross motor skills.

Vocabulary

Introduce: big, fast, diameter, length, slow, small, and speed.

If appropriate, introduce more complex vocabulary, such as: displacement, gradient, speed, velocity, and volume.

 Health & Safety

Check allergies first and take precautions to contain any mess which could represent a slip hazard.

What to do:

1. Arrange two different-length/diameter tubes at an angle and, on the count of three, children can drop the toy cars down the tube to see which appears first.

2. Increase suspense by making a 'Wheeeeee!!!' noise together as the car moves down the tube. Invite them to guess which car will win the race.

3. Say 'I wonder what will happen if we use these objects instead..?' and, taking it in turns, the children can experiment with picking objects for their own races and predicting which objects and tubes will work best and why.

4. Children can experiment with making their own tubes from rolled-up newspaper to create the optimum length, diameter and gradient.

Top tip ⭐

Ensure that at least some of the selected objects fit in all the tubes offered to younger children.

Drop, plop, slop

What you need:

- A collection of non-breakable every day or natural objects
- A one metre stick or tape measure
- A bowl of flour and a bowl of water
- Stopwatches, scales, cameras (optional)

Top tip ⭐

Vary with bowls of maize, peanuts, sand, or paint for fun mark-making. Invite children to find their own natural treasures, such as leaves, feathers and seed pods to experiment with.

Taking it forward

- Invite the children to suggest variations, such as changing the types of objects or contents of the bowls.
- Drop the objects in three containers of paint instead – each containing a primary colour, i.e. red, yellow, and blue. Cover the area with paper first for creating Jackson Pollock-inspired paintings, or for inspiring a focus on colour mixing. Be sure to wear protective clothing or old clothes.

What's in it for the children?

Introduces scientific and mathematical concepts such as cause and effect, gravity, displacement, speed, and momentum. Develops problem solving and supports tool use.

Vocabulary

Introduce: gravity, speed, and weight. If appropriate, introduce displacement and momentum.

What to do:

1. Select three non-breakable items from the collection: one heavy, one light, and one large.

2. Position the two bowls side by side on a soft surface, ideally outside on grass.

3. Pick three objects and pass these round so all the children can feel their weight and compare them, weighing them if they wish.

4. Invite three children to stand in a row, each holding one of the objects at an agreed height, e.g. one metre.

5. Invite the children to predict what will happen when the three objects are dropped.

6. On the count of three, the objects are dropped, so that one falls in the water, one in the flour and one on the grass. The rest of the children sit or lie on the grass to watch, time or film them to find out which object lands first.

7. Talk about what happened and if, and how, this differed from what they expected. Measure which object made the most mess and discuss why.

8. Try again with different children and objects, or bowls filled with different contents.

➕ **Health & Safety**
Play on a non-slip surface and check allergies if using flour.

Eggs and spoons

What you need:

- A varied assortment of different-sized and shaped spoons, e.g. measuring, salt, wooden, draining and teaspoons and scoops
- A variety of different-sized eggs. Again, pick a range of colours, patterns and properties, e.g. solid, opaque, transparent, metal, woollen, wooden, plastic, rubber, paper, etc.

Top tip ⭐

Try to resist the temptation of speeding up children's thinking or intervening by suggesting the structured activity. Instead, invest time in picking an enticing variety of eggs and spoons for experimentation.

Taking it forward

- Set up an obstacle course for the children to transport their eggs over.
- Alternatively, position four containers in a line or in different corners of the room, each with a child standing next to it. Working in teams, the challenge is for the first person to transport their egg to the first container and the second child to pick up the egg and take it to the next container, and so on, in a relay egg and spoon race.

What's in it for the children?

Develops problem solving, thinking skills, cooperative working, and fine and gross motor skills. Introduces movement.

Vocabulary

Introduce: big, carry, drop, easy, egg, fall, hard, heavy, light, pass, small, spoon, transport.

What to do:

1. Simply arrange the eggs and spoons in a basket or on the floor, and sit back and watch how children interact with the objects.

2. Some children will sort the eggs or spoons; others will use the spoons to pick up the eggs, balance the eggs on the spoons, or transport the eggs with the spoons.

3. Notice and record how each child interacts with and uses the objects to guide future planning.

4. If appropriate, support children's thinking by highlighting the different qualities/properties of the eggs and spoons, e.g. 'So the large heavy egg fell off the tiny spoon'.

5. If appropriate, after plenty of time to freely explore the resources, invite them to have an egg and spoon race whereby the children pick their own egg and spoon. Talk about what happened and which eggs worked best with which spoons and why.

✚ Health & Safety

Children should wear shoes and play on a soft surface, to minimise dropping hazards.

Fee fi fo thumb

What you need:

- Some commonly-shaped objects, such as cubes, sphere, cylinder, pyramid, square, circle (woollen, rubber, wicker and metal balls and cuboid boxes and tins would work well)

- A feely bag (e.g. a PE bag or pillow case) ideally large enough for the selected objects and for children to be able to put their whole arms in

Taking it forward

- Young children can spot curves and straight lines first, or as an alternative.

- Older children can spot 3D shapes such as sphere, cube, cuboid, prism.

What's in it for the children?

Develops shape recognition and an understanding of the characteristics of shapes – the foundations for mathematics and writing. Supports fine motor skills, turn-taking and self-esteem as children take risks by feeling in the bag. Hones an awareness of rhyme and tactile perception.

Vocabulary

Introduce: straight, sides, lines, curves, square, circle, rectangle, cuboid, sphere, cylinder.

What to do:

1. Sit in a circle, passing the feely bag round like 'pass the parcel'. As it passes say 'Fee fi fo thumb, let's feel some shapes and have some fun!'

2. The child holding the bag when this ends feels inside as you continue the rhyme: 'Feel each shape with finger and thumb; can you spot a circle one?' The child then feels in the bag to try to find a matching shaped object.

3. Look together at the object selected and, if the right shape, confirm 'you have found the circle shape.' If it isn't the right shape, summarise 'you have found a shape with a curve and a straight side'; then invite the child to feel or look in the bag again, supporting with prompts: e.g. 'So, we're looking for a shape that's round with no straight sides or pointy edges. Can you feel a shape like that?'

4. Repeat with passing the bag as you say the rhyme, changing the shape each time.

Top tip

As you say the rhyme, build up the shape name in a TV style to create suspense. Support with questions and prompts, summarizing knowledge if needed, e.g. 'So, can anyone spot a circle/sphere in the room..? So, it has curved sides...Can you feel an object in the bag with curved sides?' Invite the children to suggest the shape for the rhyme and, if possible, to help each other give clues and find the right shape.

Feely basket

What to do:

1. Take the children on a 'texture walk' outdoors to introduce opportunities to feel a variety of textures. If appropriate, children can explore in pairs, taking it in turns to lead their partner or close their eyes to touch things.

2. Introduce a range of texture words to help enrich the experience.

3. After ample time, or on another occasion, gather around the basket, ideally outdoors, and invite them to each pick an object to feel. Once they have explored several objects, invite them to pick one to share how it feels and what they like or dislike about it.

4. Circulate the objects so that everyone can feel and add their own describing words.

5. Experiment with how some materials change depending upon whether left in the sun or the cold, or if held in the hand.

Taking it forward

- Older children can create their own similes, e.g. rough like elephant skin.
- Alternatively, challenge them each to come up with a different describing word for each object, valuing made-up words too.

What's in it for the children?

Provides sensory stimulation and introduces lots of language.

Vocabulary

Introduce: bumpy, prickly, smooth, rough, scary, soft, warm, cold, hard, springy, temperature.

 Health & Safety

Children should wash their hands after exploring outside.

Feely sock

What you need:

- One or more large thick socks
- A selection of interesting objects including different sizes, shapes, textures, noise appeal and density
- Stopwatch (optional)

Top tip

Introduce humour by exclaiming, e.g. 'Oh I hope that was the clean sock!' and theatrically smelling it to make sure.

Taking it forward

- If playing with younger children, let them look at the objects first before putting the objects in the sock(s).
- Older children can do the same; then race in teams to work out their objects first.
- Add scented interest with a lavender sachet, or an orange pricked with a fork.
- Add auditory interest by including an egg timer or bell.

What's in it for the children?

Encourages turn-taking and sensory awareness. Develops descriptive language.

Vocabulary

Introduce: Feel, hard, heavy, hollow, light, outline, press, shape, soft, solid, turn etc.

What to do:

1. Fill the sock with up to ten of the objects and sit in a circle with the children.

2. Pass the sock around, giving each child enough time to feel the objects through the sock.

3. Sing together 'Feel the sock wriggle and move, wriggle and move, wriggle and move. /Feel the sock wriggle and move/ Can you feel it?' to the tune of 'London Bridge'.

4. If playing with several children, or you know they will struggle to wait, pass more than one sock at the same time, or have one sock each to keep them occupied.

5. Support with questions such as 'Does it feel soft/hard?' while summarising their facts.

6. Continue until all the children have felt the sock(s) and ask if they can guess what any of the objects were. Explore what led them to guess and why; then open the sock to see what the objects were. Talk about any surprises.

50 fantastic ideas for treasure baskets

Fishy shapes

What you need:

- Some common 2D- and 3D-shaped objects, (e.g. circle, square, sphere, cylinder that can be put in water without spilling – wood, metal and rubber would work well)
- A shallow or see-through water tray or paddling pool
- Magnets, nets, tongs, fishing rods
- Stop clock or watch
- Word cards, e.g. circle, square, sphere, cylinder, straight line, curved line

What to do:

1. Fill the tray/pool with tepid water, ideally positioned outside.

2. Put the selected objects in the water.

3. Make a set of cards, each with a different shape drawn and written on it, and place face down in a pile.

4. One at a time, children pick a card and use the magnets, nets, or tongs to catch a matching object. If they successfully match the card and object, they keep both; if not, the card returns to the bottom of the pile and the object to the water.

5. Support the children in discovering when to use the magnets and other tools. Talk about what works, what doesn't work, and why.

6. When all the objects have been 'caught', the children can count their catch to see who has the most.

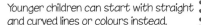

Top tip

Younger children can start with straight and curved lines or colours instead.

Taking it forward

- Children can play in teams, each with the same cards, with the challenge of finding matching objects the quickest.

- Add bubbles, food colouring or ice cubes to the water for visual and sensory interest and intrigue.

What's in it for the children?

Develops mathematical thinking, an understanding of properties, problem solving, turn-taking, hand-eye coordination and fine and gross motor skills in a hands-on fun way.

Vocabulary

Introduce: attract, catch, curve, fishing rod, line, magnets, net, object, repel, scoop, straight, tongs and twist.

 Health & Safety

Always closely supervise water play.

Fill and pour

What you need:

- A range of jugs, containers, tea strainers, sieves, and funnels. These should include different sizes, shapes, colours, and properties, i.e. metal, wooden, rubber and stone

- A selection of spoons, including different sizes, shapes and materials

- A large tray of dry sand (or smaller individual trays) containing a mix of sand, glitter, dried rice, dried lentils, pea shingle or similar

- A large tray of tepid water, with ice cubes, pea shingle and glitter (all optional)

What to do:

1. Arrange the objects and tools next to the tray and simply watch as the children freely explore the resources.

2. Play alongside if invited; otherwise use this as a valuable opportunity to observe, notice and record children's play. Be careful not to influence play. Take the children's lead as to whether to leave discussion until the end of the activity to avoid interrupting thinking or calm time.

3. At the end of play, or if more appropriate during play, discuss what the children discovered or any questions that emerge, using a range of positional, action and describing words.

✚ Health & Safety

If needed, first agree some play rules for containing spillages, or better still play outside. Always supervise water play.

Top tip ★

Use visual cues, such as traffic lights, to help children plan their time and prepare to end the activity. On its own, dry sand has limited play and learning value. By adding the other ingredients, it increases learning opportunities as children discover how different resources 'behave' when poured and what fits and doesn't in the sieves and jugs.

Taking it forward

- Substitute the dry mix for water, adding food colouring, glitter, scent, or ice cubes for sensory interest.

- Substitute the water for a dry mix instead, using sand, dried rice, glitter, gems or coloured stones, dried lentils, or pea shingle. Offer jugs of water with the sand for a focus on change and more fine and gross motor movements.

What's in it for the children?

Provides opportunities for exploring transporting and enclosure schemas. Develops mathematical and scientific language and thinking. The free focus and calming resources support well-being and self-occupation.

Vocabulary

Introduce: in, on, volume, capacity, big, small, same, different, shake, inside, full, empty, pour, transfer, trickle, splash, plop, gravity.

floating numbers

What you need:

- A selection of everyday objects that can be put in water without being ruined. If possible, sort these with the children to support their critical thinking

- Shallow, see-through water tray or paddling pool filled with tepid water

- Nets, magnets, tongs, toy fishing rods

- 3D wooden or plastic numbers in a bag, or make your own number cards between one and ten (one and twenty if older children)

- Sticky coloured dots (optional)

What to do:

1. Put the objects in the water with the nets and tools arranged nearby. The children take it in turns to pick a number, or take a card off the pile. Their challenge is to 'catch' the matching number of objects; so, if the number 3 is selected, they need to scoop out three objects.

2. Support the children, if needed, in deciding which of the tools to use and why, e.g. magnets will only work with the metal objects.

3. Add interest by challenging them to get all the objects in one or two 'scoops'.

4. Add bubbles, ice cubes, gems or food colouring, or play in dried pasta, porridge oats, lentils, shredded paper, or wood shavings instead.

5. Older children can use their feet or other parts of their body to retrieve the objects instead.

Taking it forward

- Add coloured sticky dots to the objects for scoring points or colour coding which objects each child should catch.

- Older children can use +, - and = cards for simple sums.

What's in it for the children?

Reinforces an awareness of number and properties, one-to-one correspondence, fine and gross motor skills, and hand-eye coordination.

Vocabulary

Introduce: add, attract, catch, count, float, less, more, next, numbers, scoop and sink.

Health & Safety
Always supervise water play.

Top tip ⭐
Model using the language of maths.

Footy

What you need:

- Beanbags, a selection of balls, e.g. woollen, rubber, wooden and other non-breakable objects – enough for one for each child
- A basket or container

Top tip ⭐

Use positional and directional language if appropriate, such as 'on top of', 'next to'.

Taking it forward

- Older children can race in teams with the added challenge of passing the object along a line into a container.
- Introduce obstacles for them to move the object over.

What's in it for the children?

Develops foot-eye coordination, focus, concentration, and cooperative skills. Increases muscle control, balance, and an awareness of positional language.

Vocabulary

Introduce: balance, heavy, light, move, next to, on top, pass, twist, turn, underneath etc.

 Health & Safety

Remove any sharp hazards and play on a soft floor in case the children lose their balance

What to do:

1. Children take off their shoes and sit in a circle on the floor around the objects. Invite them to warm up by picking up an object with their toes and putting it in the basket

2. Move the basket and all but one beanbag to one side, and explain that you are going to place a beanbag on your feet and pass it to the next child. The challenge is to pass the beanbag round the circle using only your feet. (Challenge older children to do so without dropping it.)

3. Talk about how easy or difficult they found it; then invite them to pick another object from the basket to try.

4. Add interest by theatrically counting each time the object is successfully passed without being dropped. Increase challenge by passing more than one object at a time.

5. Invite the children to suggest other appropriate parts of the body to try instead.

Guess and see

What you need:

- A selection of familiar objects commonly associated with different rooms in the house (e.g. plug and flannel for bathroom, egg cup and pastry brush for kitchen, mini terracotta pot for the garden, etc.)

Top tip ⭐

Sing to the tune of Frère Jacques: this will appeal to auditory learners.

Taking it forward

- Change the end of the rhyme to 'Guesses three' and challenge the children to work together to decide which three guesses to try.

- Play with foraged treasures such as shells, leaves, seed pods and stones; and animal puppets for a forest, farm or seaside-themed game instead.

What's in it for the children?

Develops problem solving, cooperative working and thinking skills. Supports language.

Vocabulary

Introduce: challenge, design, home, house, guess, mystery, problem, rooms, solve, use, etc.

➕ Health & Safety

Wash hands after playing with foraged natural treasures.

What to do:

1. Arrange the objects for the children to see: then pick an object (in your mind) and sing: 'I've picked an object, I've picked an object. What can it be? What can it be? Can you guess what I've picked? Can you guess what I've picked? Let us see! Let us see!'

2. Give the first clue: 'We find this in the kitchen' and invite them to guess which of the objects you have picked, challenging older children to do so with as few guesses as possible.

3. Alternatively, the group can ask lots of closed questions (in the style of Who/What am I?) and the picker answers: 'Yes' or 'No'.

4. Once the object has been correctly guessed and you've talked about what the object is and how they think it is used, simply repeat with another picker and object.

Guess the object

What you need:

- Ten everyday or natural objects that children will recognise, such as an egg cup, plug, spoon, comb, and chain. These should be picked for their different size, shape, texture, weight, etc.

- A feely bag

Top tip ⭐

Offer funny sunglasses instead of children closing their eyes as they feel in the bag.

Taking it forward

- Put all the objects in the bag except one, with the challenge of finding which object is missing.

- Add an extra object or toy to the feely bag for the children to spot the 'intruder'.

What's in it for the children?

Develops sensory awareness, fine motor skills, trust and turn-taking. Supports listening skills, problem solving and vocabulary.

Vocabulary

Depending upon the choice of objects, this introduces a wealth of adjectives such as bumpy, furry, prickly etc.

 Health & Safety
Never insist that a child closes their eyes.

What to do:

1. Arrange the objects on the floor and invite the children to say what they think each object is and why. Invite the children to look at and explore the objects.

2. If the children do not instinctively begin exploring the objects, simply model picking up objects to feel and manipulate: it is likely that the children will then follow suit. Don't be tempted to rush this important stage, as depending upon the selected objects, this activity heightens children's focus on characteristics such as texture, size, weight, heat, coldness, and conductivity.

3. Ask the children to cover their eyes while you hide one of the objects in the feely bag.

4. One at a time, the children feel in the bag (closing their eyes if wished) as they try to guess which object it is.

5. Repeat, with the children taking it in turns to pick which object to hide and feel in the bag.

Hidden numbers

What you need:

- **Select five or ten treasure-like objects** (e.g. a terracotta pot, necklace, stone, etc.)
- **A variety of brushes and spoons**
- **Fabric feely bag**
- **Shallow sand tray**
- **Wooden, plastic, or stone tactile numbers or number cards from one to ten** (or one to five if young children)
- **Magnets, string** (optional)

What to do:

1. Hide the selected objects in the sand tray.
2. Arrange the brushes and spoons from the basket next to the tray for an archaeological dig.
3. Talk about what an archaeological dig is (looking at photos or following a visit if possible) and how important it is to carefully avoid breaking the treasures!
4. Put the numbers/cards in the feely bag and invite children, one at a time, to pick out a number. The challenge is to carefully use the brushes and spoons to unearth the matching number of objects in the sand tray. Once children have dug up the right number of objects, they rebury them for the next go.
5. Add surprise objects like plastic dinosaurs and gems and provide string for older children to divide up the sand tray like an archaeological dig.

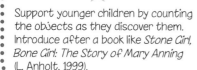

Top tip ⭐

Support younger children by counting the objects as they discover them. Introduce after a book like *Stone Girl, Bone Girl: The Story of Mary Anning* (L. Anholt, 1999).

Taking it forward

- Increase the number of objects or introduce simple sums for older children.
- Bury metal objects only for a metal detecting dig, or a mix including metal and let the children work out which objects the magnets attract.

What's in it for the children?

Sand is a wonderfully sensory and relaxing media, and this activity helps cement mathematical understanding about one-to-one correspondence and counting in a physical hands-on way.

Vocabulary

Introduce: add, archaeological dig, attract, heavy, less, light, magnets, more, numbers palaeontologist, repel.

Hoopla doopla

What you need:

- A selection of objects that are either common 3D shapes or have been picked to appeal to the children
- Paper plates with scissors and glue, plastic hoops or quoits
- Chalk or string, coloured stickers (optional)
- Tape measure

Top tip ⭐

Use positional and directional language. Provide plastic hoops as well, so the children can compare their designs and performance.

Taking it forward

- Provide coloured stickers for the children to introduce their own points system and chalk or paper for them to record the scores.

- Rearrange the objects in a circle for the hoops to land in instead. Introduce measuring opportunities such as awarding points for the furthest hoopla or setting out the course.

What's in it for the children?

Develops fine and gross motor skills and hand-eye coordination. Promotes turn taking, problem solving and mathematical language.

Vocabulary

Introduce: accuracy, around, direction, far, furthest, hoop, hoopla, long, near, next to, shapes, short, toss, throw.

Health & Safety

Agree throwing rules and avoid problems by playing outside.

What to do:

1. If the children are making their own hoops, they can cut out the centre of two paper plates and glue them together, decorating if they so wish. Encourage them to find a space to practice throwing their hoops and make any design modifications to improve speed or accuracy.

2. Arrange the selected objects in a line on the floor and draw a chalk throwing line, depending upon the children's age, between one metre and three metres away. Start off with the throwing line closer to the objects, gradually moving it further away.

3. The children take it in turns trying to hoopla the objects. Cheer if successful, and talk about their ideas for improving accuracy, if appropriate.

4. Add interest and challenge by rearranging the objects so some are further away and more difficult. The children could pick and name which object or shape they are going to aim for, reinforcing shape names (or colours) as they do so.

Hot properties

What you need:

- A selection of wooden, metal, textile, plastic, glass, and rubber objects (You will need several of each material. Try to pick as varied objects as possible.)

- Some child-sized tools, if appropriate

What to do:

1. Gather the children around the objects and explore together what they think the objects are made of. Be sure to listen to and value children's thoughts and logic, as this will provide an important insight into their existing understanding of the world.

2. Sort the objects together according to their material, e.g. wood, metal, etc., discussing each object and supporting their working theories as they do so.

3. Start with wood, asking: 'Does anyone know where wood comes from?'; then go outdoors to explore a tree, noticing the texture of its bark, the sounds and feel of the leaves, the spectacle of looking up at its canopy. Talk about the different textures and parts of the tree and notice the rings in a cut log.

4. Look at the wooden objects and talk about what parts of the tree they might have been made from. Research the different properties of different woods and what types of wood are used for making what types of objects.

5. Listen to children's knowledge and understanding so that you can help them fill any gaps and consolidate learning, if needed. Try to identify family crafts or tradespeople to invite in to share their expertise.

6. Invite the children to pick another material from the objects to explore further through books, the Internet, experiments, or a visit.

SPAGHETTI MEASURER

WOODEN TOP-UP

Taking it forward

- Provide a range of investigative tools and resources, such as magnifiers, torches, scales, magnets, and woodworking tools, if appropriate, for children to follow up on their seeds of inquiry.

What's in it for the children?

Supports children's understanding of the world, and change, and develops critical thinking, problem solving and creativity. Develops gross and fine motor skills.

Vocabulary

Introduce: attract, carpenter, float, heat conductor, metal, metal worker, plastic, properties, repel, rubber, sink, wood etc.

Top tip ⭐

Don't assume that children will know, for example, that the wooden objects were once part of a tree, or that magnets only attract metals.

✚ Health & Safety

Follow health and safety rules if working with wood or glass.

Hot potatoes

What you need:

- A selection of beanbags, balls and objects that can be safely thrown

Top tip ⭐

Supports cognitive skills by combining language and movement. Works well as an energizer or reminder of children's names.

Taking it forward

- Add excitement by playing music. When the music stops, the child holding the object says a word to describe it.
- Play in teams with more than one object being thrown.

What's in it for the children?

Develops gross and motor skills, encourages listening, turn-taking, and reinforces names. Supports vocabulary and hand-eye coordination in an energising way.

Vocabulary

Depending upon the objects, introduce lots of action and describing words.

➕ Health & Safety

Check the objects before use. If appropriate, introduce throwing rules.

What to do:

1. Sit in a circle and begin juggling a beanbag like a hot potato. Ask the children to imagine that it is a hot potato that has just come out of the oven and it is too hot to hold. You need their help passing it without dropping it on the floor. Say a child's name and theatrically throw the 'potato' to them. Continue while all the children are engaged, pretending to nearly drop it if you can.

2. Each child can select their own hot potato to juggle, and see who can keep it in the air without dropping the longest.

3. Invite them to pick a different object, but this time they say a word to describe the object like soft ball, red beanbag, etc. If the child is stuck they can simply say 'hot potato!'.

4. Take it in turns picking new objects and coming up with new rules.

Huff puff houses

What you need:

- A collection of everyday household items and natural treasures, being sure to include a colection of wiokor, wood, pottery, and stone items
- Some string, wool or PE hoops (all optional)

Top tip ⭐

Support children's thinking and cooperative skills by helping them frame the challenge and actions needed.

Taking it forward

- Provide large rolls of paper, hard hats, bricks, and wheelbarrows for a building/architect's role play.
- Make junk modelling resources available for the children to create and test their own structures as part of a focus on architecture or making earthquake proof buildings.

What's in it for the children?

Encourages sequencing, memory, and storytelling. Develops problem solving and scientific knowledge.

Vocabulary

Introduce: blow, bricks, build, cement, fall, flimsy, materials, properties, reeds, stable, stone, strong, tumble, walls, weak, wicker, wood

➕ Health & Safety

Introduce rules or do mini risk assessments if using real building resources.

What to do:

1. Sit together and talk about the story of *The Three Little Pigs* (or *The Three Little Goslings* if that is more culturally appropriate); then read the story together.

2. At the end of the story ask children what the three houses were made of – straw, wood, and brick. Explain that you are going to use the objects to recreate the houses in the story. First, they may wish to sort the objects into three piles or circles (using the string), putting the wicker items in one circle, wooden in another, and stone and pottery in another.

3. Start to retell the story using different voices for the characters. For older children, invite them to do so instead. Younger children can join in with the wolf's huff and puff words.

4. When it gets to the parts where the pigs/goslings build their houses, the children can create a tower or structure with the appropriate objects. When the wolf tries to blow the house down, on the count of three, all the children blow as hard as they can to topple the house. Repeat with the remaining houses.

5. Talk about what happened to each house and why.

Ice age fun

What you need:

- A variety of containers, ideally different sizes, shapes, and materials
- A selection of spoons and utensils (e.g. mini meat tenderisers, rolling pins or spatulas, ideally wood and metal)
- Builder's tray (or similar)
- Some plastic animals, dinosaurs, or creepy crawlies
- Glitter and powder paint (optional)
- Salt in shakers

What to do:

1. Invite the children to fill a selection of the containers with water, adding an animal or insect and glitter or colour if wished. Freeze overnight.

2. Arrange the spoons and utensils in a builder's tray or similar and add the frozen containers.

3. Challenge the children to excavate the animals using the utensils and salt provided.

4. Recreate a story, such as *The Polar Bears' Home* (L. Bergen, 2008) or *Welcome to the Icehouse* (J. Yolen, 1998), by freezing the characters for the children to rescue. Alternatively, children can create their own magical stories.

Taking it forward

- If focussing on a particular letter or sound, freeze objects that begin with that letter, e.g. a dinosaur, duck, dice, etc. for the letter 'd'. Alternatively, the focus could be on a particular colour, and the creatures, objects and paint colouring could all be the same colour.

- Freeze treasure hunt clues in separate pots for the children to excavate and solve.

- Freeze the insects or dinosaurs in egg-shaped containers instead, as these will have an extra wow factor.

What's in it for the children?

Introduces lots of hands-on problem solving, scientific thinking and fine motor movements.

Vocabulary

Introduce: change, chip, excavate, frozen, ice, lever, melt, prise, rescue, thaw, transparent.

Top tip

If cold temperatures are forecast, the children can leave the pots outside overnight to see if the water changes. Cover to avoid animal contamination.

✚ Health & Safety

Provide gloves if needed for prolonged excavation! Avoid sharp utensils.

Long and the short of it

What you need:

- A selection of different-sized containers. These should have a variety of heights and diameters and ideally include a mix of wood, metal, cardboard, wicker, and rubber

- A round basket to put the objects in

- 1m long pieces of different-coloured wool, raffia, and string

- Rulers

- Camera and clipboards (both optional)

What to do:

1. Give the children rulers to measure some straight-sided objects (in groups): pencils and tables work well. They could also take it in turns lying down or standing against a wall to be measured.

2. Ask for their help in measuring how big the basket is using the rulers – demonstrating that the circumference is the word used to describe the distance all the way round.

3. When the children have realised that rulers work best on straight objects, invite each child to pick their own 'measure' from the string, wool and raffia to explore and measure the objects with.

Top tip ⭐

Support the children in holding their measures taut, if needed.

Taking it forward

- Children could go on a measuring walk outdoors, freely measuring whatever interests them.

- Alternatively, challenge them to find the tallest, shortest, widest, or largest circumference to measure.

- They can take pictures of things they want to share with the group and record their measurements on clipboards.

What's in it for the children?

Develops an understanding of maths and measures. Supports independent learning, cooperative work, tool use and manual dexterity.

Vocabulary

Introduce: around, circle, circumference, cylinder, diameter, height, measure, tall, width, volume etc.

➕ Health & Safety

Supervise the use of the resources to avoid strangulation hazards.

Lasting impressions

What you need:

- A selection of interestingly-shaped and textured objects and natural treasures that will not be ruined when used with malleable resources

- **Plasticine, clay or playdough** (or a combination of these)

- A table mat

- **Camera** (optional)

Top tip ⭐

If possible, make the playdough together so that the children can experiment with consistency, texture, fragrance and change.

What to do:

1. Arrange the malleable resources on a covered table. Multi-coloured plasticine will offer different play and learning opportunities to a uniform colour. Clay will require more pressure and gross and fine motor skills than playdough and plasticine. Homemade playdough provides an opportunity to add colour and smell.

2. Invite the children to play freely with the objects, which, compared with plastic tools, should offer a huge range of experimentation and pattern-making potential.

3. If needed, play alongside while modelling how to use the objects to make different patterns and prints.

4. After the activity, talk about what the children did, letting them share any surprises or their favourite patterns.

5. The children can photograph their creations for a tactile display or use air dry clay so that the prints can be kept for painting or used as printing stamps.

Taking it forward

- Play a guess-the-pattern game with a child, making a pattern with an object and everyone else trying to guess which object made the pattern. Detail fascinates children, so they may be much better at this than adults.

- Give each child a piece of clay for them to create a tile, pot, or printing stamp. They can then use the texture and features of the objects to decorate their creations.

What's in it for the children?

Supports creativity and problem solving. Develops fine and gross motor strength and skills. Encourages a focus on pattern and detail and values individual choices.

Vocabulary

Introduce: imprints, malleable, mould, pattern, press, print, shape, texture, trace.

Museum muddle

What you need:

- A selection of interesting or old objects, treasures, or artefacts like those that you might find in a museum

- Pens, card for labels

- A duster or cloth

- Dressing-up clothes and books (optional)

Top tip

Initially pick objects with simple names, such as: box, tin, peg, cup, egg, ball, bag, pot. Emphasise the initial sounds of each word as you read the signs.

Taking it forward

- Add detail to encourage creativity and capture the interest of older children, e.g. a cup from which Shakespeare has drunk (or any names that they will have heard of) or a Dodo's egg.

- Older children can set up two museums and race each other to get their exhibits and labels sorted first. Provide dressing-up clothes for them to give guided tours of their museum; and books and the Internet for researching their exhibits.

What's in it for the children?

Reinforces letter sounds and simple words in a fun way. Encourages writing, problem solving and a focus on the world around us.

Vocabulary

Introduce: artefact, curators, display, exhibit, facts, history, museum, relic, signs, treasure, valuable, visitors.

What to do:

1. Talk about any museums that the children have visited (or, better still, visit one together). List the sorts of things they saw.

2. Invite them to pick some of the objects to be exhibits in their museum, and ask them what else they need for the display (e.g. signs).

3. Write together what each object is on a separate card (older children can do this themselves if you pick objects with simple names). Invite them to display their exhibits and signs, ready for visitors.

4. Pretend to be a clumsy cleaner in the museum and muddle up the signs as you dust. Help the children, if needed, to put the right signs with the right exhibits before the museum opens.

Olde shop

Top tip

Older children can talk about the play money and pricing of each object to help them decide prices. With younger children, you could be the shopkeeper instead.

Taking it forward

- Introduce simple sums and help children practise making choices.
- Invite them to pick objects for different types of shops, such as a kitchen, bathroom or gardening shop.

What's in it for the children?

Introduces mathematical language, critical thinking, language for a purpose, cooperative skills, and creativity in a fun way. Many children love transporting and enclosing objects, so this activity supports their schemas.

Vocabulary

Introduce: bargain, buy, calculate, change, sale, sell, expensive, less, money, more, price.

✚ Health & Safety

If playing with real money, always wash hands after use.

What to do:

1. Talk about what sorts of things are sold in antique shops, and invite the children to work in groups to create their own shops. Two or three shops work well.

2. Each group picks their objects and makes a shop sign and price labels to match the play money, e.g. 20p, 10p, 5p, 2p, 1p.

3. The children arrange their wares on a table or box and agree prices for each item.

4. Each shop needs one shopkeeper, so the rest of the children can be customers, using the play money to buy 'antiques' from the different shops.

5. Take it in turns playing different roles and join in as a customer.

6. Provide receipt books and dressing-up props or sale stickers for a sale.

Mystery prints

What you need:

- **A selection of different-shaped objects** (the more distinctive the shape, the better)
- **Powder paint** (ideally the three primary colours of red, yellow, and blue)
- **Black and white paper and sugar paper**
- **Flour sifters, tea strainers, sieves, and spoons**
- **Pipettes or squirty bottles of water**
- **Bicarbonate of soda and vinegar**
- **Aprons and floor covers**

Taking it forward

- Lay sugar paper on the ground outside on a sunny day. Position a selection of objects on this and return after several hours to see what has happened. Experiment with how long the objects need to be left to create the desired effect. Play a 'guess-the-object game' with the mystery prints.

- Explore other types of patterns created by the objects, for example by projecting an image onto a wall with a torch, or by viewing on a light table.

What's in it for the children?

Develops creativity and encourages a focus on detail. Explores change and inspires problem solving.

Vocabulary

Introduce: colours, guess, mix, mystery, outline, print, shadow, shape, sieve, sprinkle.

 Health & Safety

Be careful to avoid eyes if using vinegar.

What to do:

1. Invite each child to select an object to position on a piece of paper on the floor. They then sift or sprinkle their choice of powder paint from above, taking care not to move the object. Once they've added as many different colours as they wish they can carefully lift the object to reveal the 'print' beneath.

2. The prints can be used for a game of guessing which object made the mystery shapes. This should inspire lots of discussion, manipulation of the objects and problem solving, as the children will quickly discover how difficult it is spotting flat prints from 3D shapes!

3. Children can develop their print into a piece of transient art using other objects to create a layered effect. Alternatively, provide huge sheets of paper for a piece of group art instead.

4. If wished, they can squirt their pictures with water to see what different 'Jackson Pollack-inspired' effects they can create. They may want to experiment with removing or leaving the objects in place.

5. Alternatively, mix bicarbonate of soda with the powder paint and squirt vinegar instead of water, to create amazing fizzing pictures.

Top tip ⭐

If children prefer the smell, they can use lemon juice instead of vinegar.

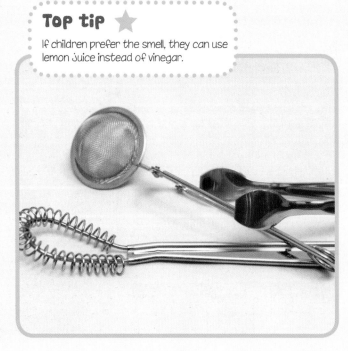

Paint pots

What you need:

- **Interestingly-shaped everyday objects and natural treasures** (low cost items, in case they are ruined)
- **A selection of paint** (either ready mixed or powder paint)
- **White paper**
- **Aprons and floor covering**

Top tip

Expect to be 'wowed' by children's fascination for and noticing of details.

Taking it forward

- Children can play a game of 'guess-the-mystery-object' that created the print.
- Challenge the children to see how many different types of patterns they can create from a single object.
- Use the objects in wet sand for more pattern-making.

What's in it for the children?

Develops creativity, fine and gross motor skills and an awareness of pattern. Encourages cooperative working.

Vocabulary

Introduce: abstract, colour, design, mystery, outline, pattern, print, repeat, zigzag.

 Health & Safety
Plan for spillages to avoid slip hazards.

What to do:

1. Cover a table or the floor and arrange the objects next to the paint. Invite the children to explore the resources, noticing and recording how they use them. If appropriate, play with the objects and paint alongside, creating your own abstract print.

2. In the absence of brushes, the children will naturally experiment by using their fingers and the objects for pattern-making.

3. If appropriate, provide a large 'canvas' for them to create their own piece of group art.

4. Ideally, do this outside so that the children can make lots of mess and forage for just the right treasure whilst painting.

5. Talk about their creations, and which objects they enjoyed using, and why. Share any surprises.

peep holes

What you need:

- A shoe box or tissue box
- A selection of interesting objects that the children will recognise from home (e.g. plug, comb, egg cup, etc.)
- Some lace material, tissue paper or tracing paper
- Scissors, sticky tape, or elastic bands
- Mirrors, binoculars, colour paddles, etc.

Top tip

Shaking it adds to the sensory appeal of holding the box and looking through the peep hole.

What to do:

1. Make a mystery box by covering the opening of a tissue box with a piece of lace or tissue/tracing paper and securing with sticky tape or elastic bands. If using a shoe box, simply make a peep hole in the lid and cover with the paper or lace.

2. Arrange the objects for the children to look at and explore. After plenty of time, secretly put one of the objects in the mystery box and ask: 'Who'd like to look in the box to try to guess what's in there?' Shake the box as you pass it to the first child.

3. Use 'I wonder…' statements, like 'I wonder what it is..?' 'I wonder how we can find out..?' 'Can you see anything?' Help them sort and summarise the information as clues, e.g. 'So, it's shiny and round and makes a thud when you shake it.'

4. The child can guess the object before opening the box to see what it is. Talk about any surprise discoveries.

5. Repeat with another child and object, or as a variation pass the box around the whole group and inviting guesses from all the children.

Taking it forward

- The peep hole helps narrow our focus, making us see details differently. Provide other related resources, such as magnifiers, colour paddles, DIY colour swatches, a kaleidoscope, diffractors and binoculars for children to explore with, inside and outside.

- Children can make their own pin-hole cameras to explore seeing the world differently.

What's in it for the children?

Great for problem solving, taking a different perspective and exploring change.

Vocabulary

Depending upon the objects chosen, this introduces lots of describing words.

✚ Health & Safety

Supervise use of scissors.

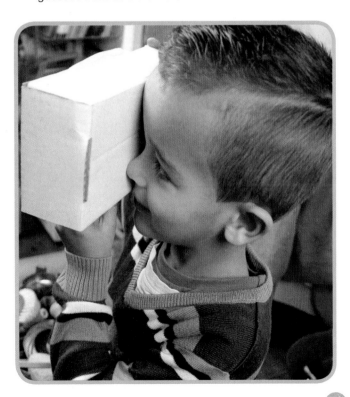

Rhythmic stories

What you need:

- A good selection of about 30 or more sensory-rich and interesting objects and treasures. These should include utensils that will make good 'beaters' and a mix of materials, especially wood and metal

- A basket for the objects

Top tip ⭐

Ensure that you have several wooden and metal objects, as well as utensils that can be used as beaters, so children can experiment with different sounds.

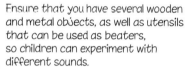

Taking it forward

- Read a familiar story together like *We're Going on a Bear Hunt* (M. Rosen, 1989) or *We're Sailing to Galapagos* (L. Krebs, 2005) using the objects to accompany the story.

- Explore the children's ideas for recreating the sounds of different animals – real or imaginary.

What's in it for the children?

Develops listening and an awareness of sounds, an important foundation for language. Encourages imagination and storytelling.

Vocabulary

Introduce: bang, beat, chime, echo, listen, rhythm, sound, vibrations etc.

What to do:

1. Sit together on the floor and invite the children to explore the basket of objects to see how many different musical sounds they can make.

2. After lots of loud experimentation, explain that you are going to use the objects in the basket to create a sound story.

3. Put a chain, or similar, into a metal tin; then invite the children to close their eyes, if wished, whilst you gently turn the tin upside down like a rainstick. Ask them what the sound reminds them of, for example rain, and use this to form the start of the story.

4. Pass to a child to 'play' every time they hear the word 'rain'.

5. Invite the children to suggest other musical sounds and actions to include in the story, experimenting with the sounds made and the story direction.

6. Tell the story together with words and the instruments.

Sandy writing

What you need:

- Treasure Basket or collection of interestingly-shaped objects
- Shallow sand tray lined first with metallic paper or tin foil
- Coloured sand (optional)
- Jug of tepid water and ice cubes (optional)

Top tip ⭐

Try to use left to right movements, as this helps prepare children for reading and writing. Using objects can support a 'tactile defensive' child who can't tolerate touching sand. If this is the focus, try to pick spoons or utensils that are more pencil-shaped.

Taking it forward

- Provide ice cubes for children to explore patterns and mark-making in dry sand.
- Increase the scale by offering sand or paint outdoors for children to use different parts of their bodies to make patterns and letters with.
- Vary by picking simple 2D- and 3D-shaped objects that will not be ruined through wet sand. One at a time, roll, flip or plop an object in the sand. Talk about how the object moved and what sort of pattern it made. Compare the patterns made by different objects and shapes.

What's in it for the children?

Supports hand-eye coordination, gross and fine motor skills, pattern recognition and creativity. The multi-sensory approach makes emergent writing fun.

Vocabulary

Introduce: curves, flip, grainy, lines, pattern, print, roll, shape, smooth, texture etc.

What to do:

1. Arrange the sand tray and basket on the floor and invite the children to freely explore the resources.

2. After plenty of time, if appropriate, pick an object to model making patterns in the sand. Experiment with using other objects and adding water to change the consistency of the sand.

3. Again, if appropriate, use an object to write with. Try to pick a silly object, such as a ball, to make the challenge fun. Delight and marvel in the children's own patterns and letters.

4. Play a game of 'guess which object made the pattern in the wet/dry sand?'. Children are naturally creative, so prepare to be 'wowed' by their ideas and their different patterns. This will offer them opportunities to be masterful and show how creative they are. Do not be surprised if children are better than adults at this.

✚ Health & Safety

Do the activity outside, or use a mat to contain spillages and minimise slipping hazards.

Sensory stories

What you need:

- **A toy vehicle** (e.g. car, sailing boat, train)**, animal puppet or toy**
- **Collection of objects**
- **Coloured cloths picked for their fit with story themes,** e.g. blue for the sea (optional)

Top tip

Try to select the objects for their variety of properties, detail, colour and qualities, to introduce as many describing words as possible.

Taking it forward

- Children can make up their own stories or create a sensory story together by sitting in a circle and each contributing one sentence at a time.

- Make up silly stories together instead.

What's in it for the children?

This activity encourages children to touch and notice details about the objects, providing lots of calming sensory feedback. It helps develop children's imagination and creativity.

Vocabulary

Introduce: big, bumpy, cool, hard, heavy, light, prickly, scrunchy, shiny, small, soft, tiny, etc.

What to do:

1. Explain to the children that they are going to create a sensory story and invite them to pick the main character from the selection of vehicles or animal toys.

2. Ask the children to suggest where the story is set; then begin the story, modelling how to use the objects. The aim is to select objects to shape the story, so a big object gives the word 'big' in the story, and so on. As you say the words that match the object, pass the object to the children to feel. Make up your own story to suit the children's interests or, better still, make one together. The qualities and features of the selected objects will shape the story. For example: *'Once upon a time the little red sailing boat* [main character] *was bobbing around on the **big** ocean. The **bumpy*** [a shell or other bumpy object] *waves tossed the boat this way and that making Little Boat feel quite dizzy. As the **grey** clouds parted, he spotted something **round** in the distance…*

3. Older children can vary by having one storyteller with the remaining children taking it in turns to select objects and naming the describing word or characteristic for the storyteller to somehow weave into the story.

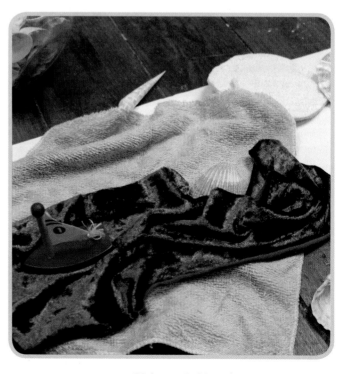

Shopping spree

What you need:

- A selection of kitchen and bathroom objects that the children will be familiar with, together with some more treasure-like objects
- Shop role-play props (e.g. till, play money, sticky dots, labels, scales, bags, etc.)
- Paper, card, and pens for creating shop signs

Top tip ⭐

Visit some local specialist shops together, to cement understanding.

Taking it forward

- If appropriate, pretend there is a gust of wind which muddles up the prices, and they need to work together to sort these before the shop opens. Alternatively, play the role of a clumsy customer who mixes up the labels.
- Provide sale stickers for the children to play around with prices.

What's in it for the children?

Supports an understanding of the world and an awareness of money and number. Introduces problem solving, marketing and creativity.

Vocabulary

Introduce: change, close, cost, customers, discount, display, expensive, labels, money, offer, open, price, sale, shop, sign, value.

➕ Health & Safety

If playing with real money, always wash hands after use.

What to do:

1. Look at the objects together and talk about what they are and where they think we might buy them.

2. If the internet or supermarket are suggested, talk about how shopping patterns have changed, inviting their input on any specialist shops that they have visited, or insight on where relatives shop.

3. Invite them to create their own shop(s), complete with signs, picking which objects they want to 'sell'.

4. Provide price labels for them to agree and write prices on, supporting them, if needed, to develop a pricing strategy.

5. The children take it in turns to be shopkeepers and customers.

Silly stories

What you need:

- A collection of interesting natural and household objects, picked for their variety of uses, sensory interest and familiarity
- A bag for the objects

Taking it forward

- Support older children in making up their own silly stories by picking three objects from the selection as central characters in a nonsense story. It could be as simple or silly as they like, e.g. 'Peter **Pinecone's** favourite hat was a big round squidgy hat [a *plug*] which he loved to wear to parties with his favourite coat [a *flannel* or *cloth*] (model putting the **plug** on his head and wrapping the cloth round his shoulders).

What's in it for the children?

Inspires creativity, divergent thinking and language. Supports memory and sequencing.

Vocabulary

Introduce: after, beginning, characters, end, funny, middle, next, then, silly, story.

> **Top tip** ⭐
>
> Remember that the sillier the story, the funnier children are likely to find it.

What to do:

1. Sit in a circle with the children and introduce the fun memory game, *'I went on holiday and I packed…'* which they may already be familiar with. Explain that, instead of just saying words, they are going to take it in turns picking the objects from the bag.

2. The children say together the introductory phrase (and subsequent object names) while the picker feels in the bag. When they get to the end of the list, the picker reveals the next object with a flourish and names it. Each time an object is selected and named, the children line it up in front of them as a memory aid. The bag then passes to the next child to repeat the process.

3. Vary with *'I went to the shops and bought…'*; *'For my Birthday I was given…'*; *'I made a cake with…'*, or other story openers that the children suggest.

4. Invite the children to add their own foraged natural treasures to the bag.

Singing circles

What you need:

- A sensory-rich assortment of objects including a variety of shapes, colours, materials, textures and details
- A bag large enough for the selected objects and the child's hands

Top tip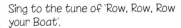

Sing to the tune of 'Row, Row, Row your Boat'.

What to do:

1. Sit in a circle and sing together the song *'Pass, pass, pass the bag gently round and round. When we stop its time to look and see what has been found.'* The child holding the bag when the music stops picks an object from the bag and gives a word to describe it, e.g. bumpy, shiny, hard.

2. They put the object back in the bag and repeat the song with a new picker and object.

3. Children can choose whether to look or just feel in the bag.

4. Challenge them to feel and pick up the object with their feet instead.

Taking it forward

- Older children can play a version where they think up all the ways each object can be used, e.g. a wooden spoon could be an ice-cream, microphone, or magic wand. Children can say or mime each use. Encourage practical and nonsensical uses to increase creative thinking.

What's in it for the children?

Develops turn-taking, language and creativity. Promotes sensory awareness.

Vocabulary

Introduce: bumpy, hard, objects, prickly, purpose, rough, shiny, smooth, soft, uses etc.

Sink or swim

What you need:

- A collection of everyday or natural objects that won't be ruined in water
- Shallow or see-through water tray or paddling pool filled with tepid water
- Toy duck, boat, and stone
- Stopwatch or timer (optional)

Top tip

Add ice cubes, glitter, food colouring, scent or bubbles to the water for extra sensory interest.

Taking it forward

- Have a contest to see which team's object floats the longest. Support them in developing their thinking about which objects to pick and why.
- Make a simple graph to record the results of each experiment.
- Go on a sink or float walk to predict and test different objects and natural treasures.

What's in it for the children?

Children are introduced to mathematical and scientific language and thinking. They have the opportunity to experience the hugely-satisfying and calming nature of water play.

Vocabulary

Introduce: area, float, heavy, heavier, light, lighter, material, properties, sink, surface, volume.

✚ Health & Safety

Always closely supervise water play.

What to do:

1. Sort the objects with the children, removing any objects that would be ruined in water, e.g. cardboard.

3. Allow plenty of time for the children to freely explore the objects.

4. Introduce the toy duck and ask them what they think will happen when it is put in water.

4. Repeat with the boat and then talk about what they predicted and what actually happened.

5. Take it in turns picking objects and guessing whether they will sink or swim (float). After each experiment, talk about what happened and any surprises.

6. Older children can create labels for sorting the objects according to whether they sink or float.

7. Invite the children to test their ideas with other objects or natural treasures by making other heavy, light, metal, big and small objects available.

Snappy soup

What you need:

- **An assortment of spoons** (try to include different sizes, materials and shapes)

- **A large saucepan or cauldron** (the older and more characterful, the better)

- **Two sets of 3D letters** (wooden, stone or plastic)

- **Some plates and a couple of pots to use for adding pretend seasoning** (these could contain sand – optional)

Top tip

Add theatricality by carefully passing the 'hot' pan (with a cloth) around the group for each child to stir. Play after reading together *Pumpkin Soup* (H. Cooper, 1998).

Taking it forward

- Young children may struggle to spoon out just one letter, in which case simply name together all the letters. Older children can link the spilt letters to the name of different soups, so b for broccoli soup, p for pumpkin soup, etc. Model suggesting nonsense soups such as camel soup, to encourage divergent thinking.

What's in it for the children?

Develops fine and gross motor skills and strength, hand-eye coordination, and letter recognition in a fun way. Supports turn-taking and encourages creativity.

Vocabulary

Introduce: flavour, hot, mix, seasoning, soup, spill, spoon, stir, taste etc.

What to do:

1. Put all the letters in the pan and gather the children around.

2. Using a large spoon, theatrically pretend to stir, taste and add seasoning to the special soup (of letters). Invite the children to take it in turns stirring the soup with a large spoon.

3. When all the children have had a turn stirring, 'tasting' and adding 'seasoning' to the mixture, stir the soup again, this time 'accidentally' splashing one letter out of the pan!

4. Invite the children to name the letter, or if more appropriate, do so yourself; then suggest they play a game of snappy soup with one set of letters in the pot, the other in a pile. Children take it in turns taking a letter from the pile, then try to find the matching letter in the pot (by spooning or spilling).

5. If they find the matching letter, the children call out 'snappy soup!' and pretend to eat the soup, continuing until all the children have had one turn or more.

Snowflakes or fireworks

What you need:

- Several crocheted or lacy coasters (charity shops are great places to find these) or paper or foil cake doilies if unavailable
- Coloured paper (black will work best)
- Flour or icing sugar
- Powder paint, glitter, bicarbonate of soda and vinegar (optional)
- A sieve, tea strainer or flour sifter
- Aprons and floor covering

Top tip

The white and colourful versions of this activity would work brilliantly as part of a focus on winter, snow, fireworks, change or spring flowers.

Taking it forward

- Provide squirty bottles filled with water for the children to squirt at their colourful prints and turn into shooting fireworks. Add bicarbonate of soda to the powder paint and replace the water in the bottles with vinegar for fizzing fireworks. Talk about the science behind the experiment.

What's in it for the children?

Provides sensory awe and wonder. Develops children's creativity whilst supporting fine and gross motor skills and hand-eye coordination.

Vocabulary

Introduce: dust, firework, fizz, flower, pattern, print, shape, sift, snowflake, squirt etc.

What to do:

1. Spread the paper on the floor (ideally outside) and gather the children round.

2. Model positioning a mat flat on the paper and carefully sifting flour or icing sugar over it. Invite children to guess what will happen if they lift the mat, then theatrically remove it (being careful not to smudge it) to reveal a delicate snowflake pattern beneath. Talk about the pattern and what it reminds them of.

3. Invite them to pick a mat to put on the paper and repeat to create individual or group transient art work, either on paper or on the floor outdoors. This will be particularly effective if it rains!

4. Vary by experimenting with what happens if they use glitter or powder paint instead.

✚ Health & Safety
Check allergies before using flour or sugar.

Tapping trees

What you need:

- A selection of spoons and long-handled objects that can be used as musical beaters. Try to include wooden and metal beaters.

Top tip ⭐

If needed, first model using the beaters appropriately with conventional musical instruments, then lead the children outside by playing the follow the leader version.

Taking it forward

■ Lead the children in a line as you play follow the leader, gently tapping objects as you pass. The children copy by tapping the same objects, beats and rhythms. Finish by gently tapping a new leader for everyone to follow.

What's in it for the children?

Encourages listening, problem solving and creativity. Helps children discriminate sounds and rhythm. Introduces fresh air and movement.

Vocabulary

Introduce: beat, echo, hollow, gentle, pitch, reverberate, rhythm, sound, tempo, vibrations etc.

✚ Health & Safety

Support the children in carrying out their own mini 'risk assessments'.

What to do:

1. Place the 'beaters' in a pile and invite the children to join you. Invite each child to pick a beater and explain that they are going to go outside to use their 'beater' to find the sounds of different things like the trees, fences, walls, floor, shed, etc.

2. Agree together some ground rules about what they can and cannot use the beaters with, and talk about what might happen if they hit things too hard.

3. Let the children explore the outside area, experimenting with different sounds and the effects created by different types of movement, speed and forces.

4. After ample time, invite them to gather round to share their favourite sounds. Talk about why they like the sound, and if, and how, they can make different sounds with the same object.

5. Explore together how the sounds change when different beaters are used instead, and talk about what they think is happening.

Terrific towers

What you need:

- An assortment of everyday objects in a variety of materials (particularly wood and metal)
- 1 metre rule, rulers, or lengths of string
- Card or whiteboard
- Camera (optional)

Top tip

Notice the children's logic as they select and order the objects.

Taking it forward

- Introduce lots of counting opportunities by challenging children to build the tallest tower with the greatest or least number of objects.
- Record the results in a simple table or pictogram.
- Use to inspire a castle role-play, adding small-world toys or props, if appropriate.

What's in it for the children?

Develops cooperative work, sequencing, problem solving, mathematical and scientific understanding. Supports fine and gross motor skills.

Vocabulary

Introduce: balance, base, different, heavy, highest, less, light, measure, more, numbers, same, tall, taller, tallest, tower etc.

✚ Health & Safety

Pick a soft but firm surface such as sand, grass or a mat, and avoid breakable objects

What to do:

1. Write the challenge on card or a whiteboard for everyone to see: 'Build a tower so tall, that it nearly reaches the sky. Then measure it quickly before it falls, to see how high it is.'

2. Invite the children to use the selected objects to build their towers, either together or in two teams.

3. Support the children's problem solving as they develop strategies for increasing the height of the tower, or ways of measuring it without knocking it over.

4. Once measured and recorded, they can knock their towers down with scrunched-up paper balls.

5. Talk about what they did, what they expected to happen, and any changes that they made.

Tasty treats

What you need:

- **An assortment of spoons** (try to include different sizes, materials, and shapes)
- **A large saucepan or cauldron** (the older and more character the better)
- **A set of 3D letters** – ideally wooden or metal
- **Some play plates, knives and forks**

Top tip ⭐

Where possible, introduce humour, e.g. 'I didn't know "cabbage jelly" was your favourite!' Give children permission to think creatively by picking creatively for yourself, e.g. z for zebra nuggets!

Taking it forward

- Once they have several letters on their plate, older children can try to make up their own real or nonsense words, using a pot of vowel letters for 'seasoning'.
- Children can come up with their favourite food, e.g. jelly, and then use the spoon to find the matching letter instead.

What's in it for the children?

Supports letter recognition and an awareness of letter sounds. Encourages turn-taking, creativity and wellbeing.

Vocabulary

Introduce: consonants, food, letters, preferences, seasoning, vowels.

What to do:

1. Put the letters in the pan next to the plates and cutlery.

2. Stir the letters and say to the children that lunch is nearly ready. Explain that this magical saucepan serves up every type of food in the world.

3. Invite the children to suggest their favourite foods and why they like them; then ask who would like to try out the magical pan first.

4. Say 'Let's see what [name] has wished for today…' as the child holds out their plate to be served. Scoop a letter onto their plate and, if needed, say the name of the letter and a food beginning with that letter 'Oh look it's a b for broccoli'.

5. Children may choose to serve themselves, name the letter and suggest a food, or may need support.

6. Once each child has had one serving, ask who would like seconds.

Transient pictures

What you need:

- A selection of enticing sensory-rich objects and natural treasures
- A large white sheet, paper, or outdoor floor
- Mirrors and camera

Top tip

Support children's ability to get the most from this by first introducing them to examples of transient art. Invite them to collect their own treasures as part of a foraging trip, so that they can collect with their art project in mind.

What to do:

1. Invite the children to create their own transient artwork, either individually or in groups, using an array of objects and natural treasures.

2. This can be completely free play for the children to choose what to do, or could form part of a focus on a theme such as animals, shapes, or the seasons.

3. Provide ample time and space for the children to return to their creations and look at them from different perspectives, using the camera and mirrors as tools to help them see them from the sides, above, on the floor, etc.

4. Once finished, invite the children to photograph their creation and label it with a word or phrase. If possible, make time for them to present their creations to the group.

Class: 3 72.21

Accession No: 1S 2561

Type: 3 Wks

Taking it forward

- If appropriate, use an animation app (several free beginner-level apps are available), in groups to create moving transient art pieces. Children can then play and present these to an audience.

What's in it for the children?

Develops creativity, provides sensory stimulation, and develops fine motor skills. Introduces mathematical positional language.

Vocabulary

Introduce: abstract, change, design, direction, pattern, picture, position, shape, view, etc.

 Health & Safety

Reinforce rules about washing hands after touching natural items.

Woolly numbers

What you need:

- A selection of interesting and sensory-rich objects

- A set of A5 number cards, each with a number between 1 and 10 (or 1 to 5 if younger children)

- A selection of different-coloured wool in a variety of lengths (or PE hoops)

- Cards with +, - and = written on them (optional)

What to do:

1. Make a set of number cards and place face down in a pile. Gather the children round.

2. Arrange the items into small groups of up to five or ten, then encircle each group with a piece of wool or hoop.

3. One at a time, invite the children to take a number card from the pile and find the matching group. So, a card with the number one matches a circle containing just one object. Alternatively, children can pick a number card and create a woollen circle of objects to match this. As a group, count together the objects, reinforcing the stable order principle that numbers are always said in the same order. Check this number with the card.

4. Invite the children to form groups themselves by standing in the circle(s) to match the right number card. Vary the length of wool or size of hoops, so they need to squeeze together.

5. Add interest and challenge, if appropriate, by inviting them to find two objects with holes, three shiny objects, or to create their own woolly sums.

6. Introduce movement by positioning the circles around the room.

Taking it forward

- Invite children to suggest and create their own groupings. These could be based on colour, size, shape or preferences. Prepare to be surprised by the groupings and detail of what children spot, and be open-minded to their logic, as objects like these can be grouped in numerous ways.

- Children may enjoy using foraged treasures such as sticks, pebbles, feathers, and shells instead.

What's in it for the children?

Cements children's learning about numbers, one-to-one correspondence, ordering, sequencing, number bonds and properties in a tactile way. Encourages children's handling and manipulation of objects.

Vocabulary

Introduce: add, different, equals, less, more, pattern, same, sort, take away etc.

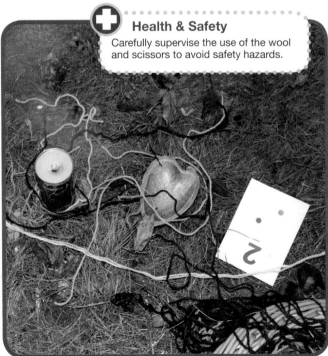

Health & Safety
Carefully supervise the use of the wool and scissors to avoid safety hazards.

Top tip ⭐

This is a great sensory way of introducing older children to number bonds to ten and reinforcing one-to-one correspondence.